Walking with God

OUR WISE COUNSELOR

Trusting God's Guidance

PHYLLIS BENNETT

NAVPRESS

OUR GUARANTEE TO YOU

We believe so strongly in the message of our books that we are making this quality guarantee to you. If for any reason you are disappointed with the content of this book, return the title page to us with your name and address and we will refund to you the list price of the book. To help us serve you better, please briefly describe why you were disappointed. Mail your refund request to: NavPress, P.O. Box 35002, Colorado Springs, CO 80935.

For a free catalog
of NavPress books & Bible studies call
1-800-366-7788 (USA) or 1-800-839-4769 (Canada).

www.navpress.com

The Navigators is an international Christian organization. Our mission is to advance the gospel of Jesus and His kingdom into the nations through spiritual generations of laborers living and discipling among the lost. We see a vital movement of the gospel, fueled by prevailing prayer, flowing freely through relational networks and out into the nations where workers for the kingdom are next door to everywhere.

NavPress is the publishing ministry of The Navigators. The mission of NavPress is to reach, disciple, and equip people to know Christ and make Him known by publishing life-related materials that are biblically rooted and culturally relevant. Our vision is to stimulate spiritual transformation through every product we publish.

© 2008 by Phyllis Bennett
Previously published as *Our Perfect Example: Following God's Ways*, Copyright 1994 by Phyllis Bennett.

ISBN-13: 978-1-60006-220-9
ISBN-10: 1-60006-220-2

Cover design by The DesignWorks Group, Tim Green, www.thedesignworksgroup.com
Cover image by Getty Images, Stuart Redler
Creative Team: Dan Benson, Karen Lee-Thorp, Reagen Reed, Darla Hightower, Arvid Wallen, Kathy Guist

Some of the anecdotal illustrations in this book are true to life and are included with the permission of the persons involved. All other illustrations are composites of real situations, and any resemblance to people living or dead is coincidental.

Unless otherwise identified, all Scripture quotations in this publication are taken from the HOLY BIBLE: NEW INTERNATIONAL VERSION® (NIV®). Copyright © 1973, 1978, 1984 by International Bible Society. Used by permission of Zondervan Publishing House. All rights reserved. Other versions used include: the *New American Standard Bible* (NASB), © The Lockman Foundation 1960, 1962, 1963, 1968, 1971, 1972, 1973, 1975, 1977, 1995; the *English Standard Version* (ESV), copyright © 2001 by Crossway Bibles, a division of Good News Publishers. Used by permission. All rights reserved. *THE MESSAGE* (MSG). Copyright © 1993, 1994, 1995, 1996, 2000, 2001, 2002, 2005. Used by permission of NavPress Publishing Group; and the *King James Version* (KJV).

Printed in the United States of America

1 2 3 4 5 6 7 8 / 11 10 09 08

CONTENTS

FOREWORD

One big difference between our current culture and that of a century ago is that the Victorians saw life in terms of roles, while we see it in terms of relationships. Real life, we say, is a matter of relationships, for roles minimize personal involvement while relationships maximize it.

In saying this, we speak more Christian truth than perhaps we realize. For real life according to the Bible means relating not just to other people but also to the personal God who made us. We live and move and exist in him, and it is both scandalous and impoverishing when we ignore him.

Who is he? The startling truth is that he is a *society*. The Father, Son, and Holy Spirit share with each other an intimate and loving relationship. Yet in the unity of their interpersonal life, they constitute a single divine being. God is they, a society and a team, and they are he, the only God there is.

A mystery? An inexplicable reality? Yes, but a life-giving one. It is our privilege not simply to acknowledge the truth of the Trinity but also to enter into Spirit-sustained relationship with the Father and the Son—a relationship which from one standpoint is *eternal life*, and from another is *knowing* God.

Knowing people involves, first, knowing facts about them and, second, making their acquaintance. How deep our relationship goes depends on how much empathy we have, how many concerns and interests we share, and how much we seek to exalt the one we love. It is the same with knowing God.

The Bible is God's communication to all who hear or read it. Through its varied contents, the Triune Lord tells us about himself and calls us to himself. A proper understanding of the Bible will focus at every point on both the information about God and the invitation to know him.

The WALKING WITH GOD series is designed to help you achieve this focus. I heartily recommend it. These studies generate vision, insight, wisdom, and devotion in equal quantities. Use them and you will be blessed.

J. I. Packer

ABOUT THE WALKING WITH GOD SERIES

Every Christian desires a deeper, more personal relationship with God. We long to know him better, to feel his presence, and to experience his power in our lives. Jesus himself tells us,

> And this is the real and eternal life:
> That they know you,
> The one and only true God,
> And Jesus Christ, whom you sent. (John 17:3, MSG)

WALKING WITH GOD Bible studies can help you build greater intimacy with God by exploring who God is and how you can know him better. Each guide focuses on a specific attribute of God, such as his love, his faithfulness, or his mercy. The studies are warm and practical and personal, yet they are firmly grounded in Scripture.

The WALKING WITH GOD series has been field tested in churches across America, representing a wide variety of denominations. This time-intensive process ensured that the guides have solid biblical content, consistent quality, easy-to-use formats, and helpful leader's notes.

The WALKING WITH GOD Bible studies are designed to be flexible. You can use the guides in any order that is best for you or your group. They are ideal for Sunday-school classes, small groups, one-on-one relationships, or as materials for your quiet times.

Because each guide contains only six studies, you can easily explore more than one attribute of God. In a Sunday-school class, any two guides can be combined for a quarter (twelve weeks), or the entire series can be covered in a year.

Each study deliberately focuses on a limited number of passages, usually only one or two, which allows you to see each passage in its context. If you would like to look up additional passages, a Bible concordance will give the most help.

The WALKING WITH GOD series will help you *discover* what the Bible says rather than simply *tell* you the answers. The questions encourage you to think and to explore options rather than merely to fill in the blanks with one-word answers.

Leader's notes are provided in the back of each book. They show how to lead a group discussion, provide additional information on questions, and suggest ways to deal with problems that may come up in the discussion. With such helps, someone with little or no experience can lead an effective study.

SUGGESTIONS FOR INDIVIDUAL STUDY

1. Begin each study with prayer. Ask God to help you understand the passage and to apply it to your life.
2. A good modern translation—such as the New International Version, the New American Standard Bible, the New Revised Standard Version, or *The Message*—will give you the most help. Questions in this guide, however, are based on the New International Version.
3. Read and reread the passage. Emphasize different words. Read the verses out loud. You must know what the passage says before you can understand what it means and how it applies to you.
4. Take your time and respond to the questions provided. In addition to the questions, always ask, "What does this mean?" and "Why does this matter?"
5. Use a Bible dictionary to look up any unfamiliar words, names, or places.

SUGGESTIONS FOR GROUP STUDY

1. Come to the study prepared. Careful preparation will greatly enrich your time in group discussion. Not only is your role in a small group to explore and expand your own understanding, but it's also to support one another.

2. Be willing to join in the discussion. The leader of the group will not lecture but will encourage people to discuss what they have learned in the passage. Plan to share what God has taught you in your individual study.

3. Stick to the passage being studied. Base your answers on the verses being discussed rather than on outside authorities such as commentaries or your favorite author or speaker.

4. Try to be sensitive to the other members of the group. Listen attentively when they speak, and be affirming whenever you can. This will encourage more hesitant members of the group to participate.

5. Be careful not to dominate the discussion. By all means participate, but allow others to have equal time. One group member may need more time to talk about what's on their mind. Be sensitive about their needs. Use good judgment and allow extra space when needed; *your* time might be the next time your group meets.

6. If you are the discussion leader, you will find additional suggestions and helpful ideas in the leader's notes at the back of the guide.

INTRODUCING
OUR WISE COUNSELOR

Recently our family hosted a dinner party, and one of our dinner guests brought a flowering plant as a hostess gift. What a delight to receive love from a guest when our goal was to express love to them.

In John 14:2, Jesus tells us that he will be our host someday in heaven, for he has gone away to prepare a place for us. But what a privilege it would be to take a gift to him when we meet him at heaven's door. Psalm 90:12 gives us an idea of what that gift might look like and how we can prepare to take that gift to him. It reads, "Teach us to number our days, that we may present to You a heart of wisdom" (NASB).

When we are coming up to a much-needed vacation, we count the days we have left to work. School children count school days left before school is out. Even department stores count the shopping days left until Christmas. But how many of us really think about making each day count until God takes us home? Are we using each day to prepare a gift that would delight him—a heart of wisdom?

The NIV states this verse a little differently: "Teach us to number our days aright, that we may gain a heart of wisdom." The word *gain* in Hebrew means "to harvest" or "to bring forth" or "to pull in." When a farmer harvests wheat, he benefits from the harvest, but so do all the people who will eat what he harvests. As we gain a heart of wisdom, we will benefit from our wisdom, but so will every other person our life touches.

The word *wisdom* in this verse in Hebrew means "skillful wisdom." The word-picture it paints for me is of a white-water rapids trip our family took last summer. As we were buffeted down the rapids in our rubber raft, there were rocks and churning water and powerful undercurrents all clamoring to take us under. It took skillful wisdom to navigate through those tumultuous currents and land us safely at the bottom of the rapids.

In the same way, when we gain a heart of wisdom, we receive the skillful wisdom we need to keep from going under in the currents of life. And that skillful wisdom not only protects us but also benefits every other person who is with us.

But we cannot gain this kind of skillful wisdom if we are not getting to know God on a daily basis. That is what this study guide is designed to do—to help us get to know the "Wonderful Counselor" and the God who gives wisdom generously (see James 1:5).

We will look at Solomon as he asks for the gift of wisdom when he could have asked for long life, success, or financial prosperity. We will discover from Isaiah that our wisdom cannot compare to God's wisdom, that his thoughts are far above our own. We will dip into Proverbs to learn that God tells us to choose wisdom over folly that we might grow wiser still. And finally we will look at the Psalms to discover that God's Word provides wisdom and guidance for every aspect of life.

Jesus sent the disciples into the world to be as "wise as serpents, and harmless as doves" (Matthew 10:16, KJV). As you seek wisdom and counsel from the Lord, may he "give you the Spirit of wisdom and revelation, so that you may know him better" (Ephesians 1:17).

Phyllis Bennett

THE GIFT OF WISDOM

When William McKinley was sworn in as president of the United States in January of 1897, he stated, "Give me now wisdom and knowledge, that I may go out and come in before this people, that is so great." What a great request to make on inauguration day!

Perhaps President McKinley took the essence of his statement from King Solomon, whom God considered to be the wisest man in all the earth. Soon after Solomon's "inauguration" as king of Israel, he made this request of the Lord: "Give your servant a discerning heart to govern your people and to distinguish between right and wrong. For who is able to govern this great people of yours?" (1 Kings 3:9).

A famous Arabian Proverb reinforces Solomon's humility and his desire to seek the gift of wisdom:

He that knows not and knows not that he knows not:
He is a fool—shun him!
He that knows not and knows that he knows not:
He is simple—teach him!
He that knows and knows not that he knows:
He is asleep—wake him!
He that knows and knows that he knows:
He is a wise man—follow him![1]

Solomon was certainly not a fool. He began his reign as king as a simple man—who knew that he knew not. 1 Kings 3 describes the first part of his life and how he sought "the gift of wisdom."

1. Think of one of the wisest people you have ever known. How have you benefited from that person's wisdom?

2. Read 1 Kings 3:1-15. What do Solomon's actions in verses 1-4 reveal to you about his character, both positive and negative?

3. What does God's statement to Solomon in his dream tell you about God's view of Solomon (see verse 5)?

4. If God said to you, "Ask for whatever you want me to give you," how would you respond? (Be honest!)

5. After giving thanks, what does Solomon request from the Lord (see verses 7-9)?

   What reasons does he give for presenting this particular request to God?

6. The Lord is pleased with Solomon's request (see verses 10-15). In what ways does God express his pleasure?

7. Why should we value wisdom and discernment more than riches, honor, and a long life?

8. Read verses 16-28. Solomon gets his first opportunity to put his gift of wisdom into effect. Pretend you are a judge in a courtroom listening to two lawyers presenting their defense. How might each lawyer have defended his client?

9. In this court scene, how does Solomon uncover the truth and express wisdom through his actions?

10. Solomon, in his role as judge, teaches us that we must be able to discern truth from falsehood. In what ways does our world encourage us to distort the truth?

11. Solomon also reveals our need for wisdom. Why is the ability to discern the truth insufficient unless it is coupled with wisdom?

12. From Solomon's life we learn that wisdom and discernment are gifts from God that can be requested (see also James 1:5). In what area of your life do you need these gifts?

SUGGESTED PRAYER

Let Solomon's prayer be a model to you as you ask the Lord for "a wise and discerning heart" in the area of your life you named in question 12. Ask God to give you a longing not for wealth or success or people's approval but for wisdom.

MEMORY VERSE

The Lord was pleased that Solomon had asked for this. So God said to him, ". . . I will do what you have asked. I will give you a wise and discerning heart, so that there will never have been anyone like you, nor will there ever be."

1 KINGS 3:10-12

WALKING WITH GOD

To grow in wisdom, keep a journal for the next week of all the situations in which you find yourself needing wisdom. Note in your journal whether you take time to ask God for wisdom or whether you forge ahead with your own ideas. Try to develop the conscious habit of asking God for the gift of wisdom, a gift he promises to give to those who ask (see James 1:5).

2

WISDOM BEYOND COMPARE

Isaiah 55

In *The Pursuit of God*, A. W. Tozer urges us to step out of our comfort zones as we follow the Lord. He encourages us to climb to spiritual heights that demand an "oxygen deficit." But he implies that in those heights we will grow accustomed to breathing the air of the Master. How might our lives be different if we were willing to be drawn to those heights on a daily basis?

I long to be the kind of person who has an impact on those around me because I'm breathing the air of the Master. Isaiah 55 encourages us all to climb to spiritual heights, to let go of our own thoughts and ways so that we might experience "God's wisdom beyond compare."

1. Describe one of the most exciting invitations you have received in your lifetime and what made it so special to you.

2. Read Isaiah 55. In verses 1-2, the Lord gives an invitation to his people. If he had written these same words to us on a party invitation, how might it have read?

You Are Invited!

Who: _____

Where: _____

When: _____

What we'll do or enjoy: _____

What to bring: _____

---

3. What things are people willing to pay money for or labor for today that Isaiah warns us will not satisfy (see verse 2)?

4. What promises does God make to the nation of Israel in verses 3-5?

Which of these promises are unique to Israel, and which (if any) are relevant to us? How are they relevant?

5. Isaiah urges God's people to "seek the Lord while he may be found" (verse 6). What must we do to seek the Lord?

What assurances does God give to those who seek him?

6. How do God's incomparable thoughts and ways contrast with ours (see verses 7-9)?

In what specific areas have you discovered that God's thoughts and ways are different from your own?

7. God encourages the evil man to forsake his thoughts (see verse 7). What kinds of thoughts interrupt your fellowship with God, keeping you from hearing his higher thoughts?

What types of thoughts are the most difficult for you to let go?

8. How is God's Word similar to "the rain and the snow" (verses 10-11)?

9. In the past few weeks, how have you seen God's Word achieve his desired purposes in your life or in the life of someone you know?

10. Verses 12-13 describe Israel's return to her homeland and the benefits that would come to the nation as people sought the Lord. But how might they also describe the benefits that come to us when we:

- seek the Lord (see verse 6):

- forsake our own ways and thoughts (see verses 7-9):

- allow the Word to take root in our lives (see verses 10-11):

11. In what present situation are you tempted to lean on your own thoughts instead of God's "wisdom beyond compare"?

12. What would it look like for you to lean on God's wisdom? What would you need to do and not do?

SUGGESTED PRAYER

Ask the Lord to help you see the situation you named in question 11 through his eyes and not your own.

MEMORY VERSE

"For my thoughts are not your thoughts,
neither are your ways my ways,"
declares the LORD.
"As the heavens are higher than the earth,
so are my ways higher than your ways
and my thoughts than your thoughts."

ISAIAH 55:8-9

WALKING WITH GOD

Ask two or three spiritually mature Christians to share with you how they discern God's higher thoughts from their own thoughts as they seek to determine God's will or hear his voice.

3

THE BENEFITS OF WISDOM

Proverbs 8

Charles Spurgeon was riding home one evening, feeling tired and depressed after a long day of preaching. Suddenly the verse, "My grace is sufficient for thee" (2 Corinthians 12:9, KJV), came to mind. He imagined himself as a tiny fish in the Thames River, drinking so many quarts of water daily that he feared he might drink the river dry. He imagined hearing Father Thames whisper in his ear, "Drink away, little fish, my stream is sufficient for thee."

He next thought of himself as a mouse hiding in Joseph's enormous granaries, worried that he might eat all the grain and die of starvation. But at his moment of deepest despair, he heard Joseph saying to him, "Cheer up, little mouse, my granaries are sufficient for you."

And finally he visualized himself climbing a lofty mountain, fearing that he might run out of oxygen before he reached the summit, when God himself spoke to him and said, "Breathe away, O man, and fill thy lungs ever; my atmosphere is sufficient for thee."

God's storehouse of wisdom is just as abundant and sufficient as his storehouse of grace. Proverbs 8 tells us that God delights to give wisdom to all who seek it.

1. Have you ever sensed the Lord calling you to seek his wisdom and not your own? If so, describe a recent experience of that.

2. Read Proverbs 8:1-21. How and to whom does Wisdom extend her call (see verses 1-5)?

3. How does Wisdom describe the characteristics of her message (see verses 6-9)?

4. What value does our world today place on the characteristics listed in verses 6-9? Explain.

5. What wrong choices can keep us from pursuing Wisdom (see verses 10-11)?

6. When has the wisdom you needed for a particular decision meant more to you than all the wealth, power, and prestige the world has to offer?

Why did it mean so much in that situation?

7. Wisdom claims to live in the same house with prudence, knowledge, and discretion (see verse 12). Define each of these terms in your own words or with the help of a dictionary.

Why is each quality a good companion to Wisdom?

8. What are some of the strong preferences and lofty claims of Wisdom (see verses 13-21)?

How have you seen one or more of Wisdom's strong preferences or lofty claims at work in our world today?

9. When have you ignored or rejected one of Wisdom's strong preferences and later regretted your decision?

10. Read Proverbs 8:22-36. We learn a lot about people from their past. What can you learn about Wisdom from her past (see verses 22-31)?

11. According to verses 32-36, how can we receive the blessings of Wisdom?

12. Why is our relationship to Wisdom a matter of vital importance (see verses 35-36)?

13. Review Wisdom's strong preferences in verses 13-21. From which of these strong preferences could you benefit the most?

    What one step can you take this week to enable Wisdom's strong preference to become your own?

SUGGESTED PRAYER

Ask God to help you acquire attitudes that accord with Wisdom, such as taking the Lord seriously (fearing him, see verse 13), hating arrogance, and so on.

MEMORY VERSE

Choose my instruction instead of silver,
    knowledge rather than choice gold,
for wisdom is more precious than rubies,
    and nothing you desire can compare with her.

PROVERBS 8:10

WALKING WITH GOD

Make a list of your own strong preferences in life by completing the sentence: "I am a person who . . ." Ask two others who know you well to add or subtract from your list.

Notice which of your strong preferences are similar to Wisdom's and which are different (see verses 13-21).

What personal preferences would you be wise to eliminate in order to become a person of greater wisdom? Ask the Lord for the courage to eliminate this strong preference from your life, thanking him for the benefits you will receive as a result.

4

CHOOSING WISDOM OVER FOLLY

In the book *A Touch of His Wisdom*, Charles Stanley tells us that "God's wisdom must be deliberately chosen. We never drift into wisdom. We must make a conscious decision to seek and receive God's divine counsel and instruction."[2]

Proverbs 9 introduces us to Wisdom and Folly personified as women. The choice is up to us concerning the woman with whom we choose to dine. We can choose to eat with Folly, or we can choose to go against our culture and dine with Wisdom. In this study we will discover why Wisdom serves a far better meal than her rival.

1. How do you go about preparing your home for others to come and visit?

2. Read Proverbs 9. What do you learn about Wisdom from the type of house she has built, the meal she has prepared, and the way she conducts herself (see verses 1-3)?

What might be her motive behind each action?

3. In verses 4-6, Wisdom extends her invitation. To whom does she extend it, and what does she promise to give them?

4. Describe someone you greatly respect who exemplifies the characteristics of Wisdom portrayed in this proverb.

5. In contrast, what do you learn about Folly from the way she conducts herself, the food she prepares, and the invitation she extends (see verses 13-17)?

6. How are those who hear Folly's invitation ignorant about her previous guests (see verse 18)?

7. What do you think it means that "her guests are in the depths of the grave" (verse 18)?

Do you think this description can apply to those who are still physically alive? Explain.

8. The imagery in this chapter is sexual, but how do the competing invitations of Wisdom and Folly get played out in other arenas, such as the workplace or in a family?

9. Both Folly and Wisdom give invitations to the simple, but only Wisdom challenges the simple to leave their simple ways. In verses 7-12, what instructions does she give about walking "in the way of understanding"?

What do you think "the fear of the LORD" (verse 10) means?

What benefits can we gain if we heed each of Wisdom's teachings?

10. Have you ever followed one of Wisdom's instructions or warnings and experienced one of her benefits? Explain.

11. As portrayed in this proverb, what one aspect of Wisdom do you most desire to become a part of your life?

12. What is one step you could take this week to enable the Holy Spirit to incorporate that aspect of wisdom into your life?

SUGGESTED PRAYER

Ask the Lord to help you take seriously the risks of heeding Folly and the benefits of dining with Wisdom. Ask him to help you recognize the voices of Wisdom and Folly in your current situation.

MEMORY VERSE

The fear of the LORD is the beginning of wisdom,
and knowledge of the Holy One is understanding.

PROVERBS 9:10

WALKING WITH GOD

One of the best ways to grow in wisdom is to read and meditate on the book of Proverbs. Because Proverbs is divided into thirty-one chapters, it is easy to complete the entire book in one month by reading one chapter a day.

Starting today, make a commitment to read through Proverbs a day at a time, making sure that you reflect on what you have read and how it applies to your life. You might also want to keep a notebook of topics that are of special interest to you, making a list of proverbs that speak to these topics.

5

GOD'S PROMISED GUIDANCE

Psalm 32

My life is but a weaving, between my God and me,
I do not choose the colors, He worketh steadily,
Oftimes He weaveth sorrow, and I in foolish pride,
Forget He sees the upper, and I the underside.
Not till the loom is silent, and shuttles cease to fly,
Will God unroll the canvas and explain the reason why,
The dark threads are as needful in the skillful Weaver's hand,
As the threads of gold and silver in the pattern He has planned.
ANONYMOUS

God longs to bless our lives with his guidance. But because we can't see the top side of the garment, we don't always appreciate his skillful weaving. In Psalm 32, David teaches us that God's hand is still on us even when we sin and choose to go our own way, as well as when God is weaving the silver and gold threads into the pattern of our lives.

1. Have you ever felt God's clear guidance in a decision you made? If so, describe that experience. If not, how do you respond when other people talk about getting that kind of guidance?

2. Read Psalm 32. Biblical writers often use repetition or parallel phrases for emphasis and to draw out different shades of meaning. What repetitive words or parallel phrases do you find in verses 1-2?

What does the psalmist's repetition or use of parallelism reveal about the blessing of forgiveness (see verses 1-2)?

3. The psalmist did not always feel so blessed. What kept him from God's blessing, and what was the painful result (see verses 3-4)?

4. According to the medical profession, many physical symptoms have their root causes in our mental outlook on life. What physical symptoms do you feel can sometimes result from deceit or unconfessed sin?

5. Has deceit or unconfessed sin ever caused one or more of these symptoms in your life? If so, what did you experience?

6. What does the psalmist's repetition in verse 5 reveal about the path to restoration and forgiveness?

7. Why do you think honest confession brings not only forgiveness but also a sense of well-being and strength?

8. How are the psalmist's experiences both a warning and an encouragement to us (see verses 6-7)?

9. What else does God promise to do for the person who is both honest and trusting (see verses 8-10)?

10. What might cause us to respond to the Lord's guidance like a horse or a mule (see verse 9)?

11. Think of a time in your own life when you acted like a horse or mule without understanding. Did God use circumstances as a "bit and bridle" to control your stupidity or rebellion? If so, talk about that experience.

12. The psalmist concludes that the blessed man can rejoice in the Lord, sing, and be glad (see verse 11). Summarize why you think he comes to this conclusion.

13. What is one area of your life in which you need God to "instruct you and teach you in the way you should go" (verse 8)?

SUGGESTED PRAYER

Thank God for his desire to counsel you and watch over you in the area of your life you named in question 13. Ask him to make you sensitive to his guidance and aware of any sin or self-deceit that blinds you.

MEMORY VERSE

I will instruct you and teach you in the way you should go;
I will counsel you and watch over you.

PSALM 32:8

WALKING WITH GOD

Examine your heart and see if there is any sin in your life you are trying to cover over. Ask the Lord to reveal it to you so that you can expose it to him. Write the sin on a small sheet of paper as an act of exposing it to the Lord. Now take a match to it or toss it in the fireplace, thanking him that you can "hide in him" and not in your own cover-up.

6

GOD'S BOOK OF WISDOM

Psalm 119:9-16,65-72

In *The Hiding Place*, Corrie Ten Boom describes her misery at being placed in a flea-infested barracks in a World War II concentration camp. Much to Corrie's disgust, her sister Betsie, upon first entering this particular barracks, began thanking the Lord for the fleas! Corrie could find no reason to thank God for the miserable little creatures. Corrie and Betsie did notice, however, that their particular barracks was rarely visited by the guards, allowing them great freedom to read portions of Scripture out loud to the women confined with them. It was weeks later when they discovered the miracle of their uninterrupted Bible study—the fleas! The guards didn't want to take a chance of getting personally infested!

How easy it is to take the Word of God for granted. Corrie and Betsie only had one copy of each of the four Gospels to share with these women who desperately needed hope. Psalm 119 motivates us to appreciate the availability of God's Word and all its richness.

1. What book besides the Bible has had the greatest impact on your life lately? How has it affected you?

2. Read Psalm 119:9-16. The psalmist is an activist. He does not let God's Word sit on a shelf collecting dust. What actions does he initiate to interact with God's Word?

3. What benefits does he expect to gain from his interaction with God's Word?

4. Have you ever hidden God's Word in your heart (see verse 11)? If so, in what ways? If not, how do you respond to the idea of making this a habit?

Has hiding God's Word in your heart ever kept you from sinning? If so, when?

5. What do "following God's statutes" and "great riches" (verse 14) have in common?

    How do they differ?

6. The psalmist devotes his energy to seeking, rejoicing in, meditating on, and delighting in God's Word. Into what activities, places, people, or things do you tend to direct your energy?

    Why do you give your energy to these things? What do you aim to get out of them?

How able are these things to meet the deepest needs of your heart? Why is that?

7. Describe what it would mean for you to interact with God's Word in each of the following ways:

- "I rejoice in following your statutes" (verse 14):

- "I meditate on your precepts" (verse 15):

- "I consider your ways" (verse 15):

- "I delight in your decrees" (verse 16):

8. Read Psalm 119:65-72. What requests does the psalmist make of the Lord (see verses 65-66)?

9. The psalmist indicates that there was a before and after period of affliction in his life (see verses 67,71-72). How does he see God using this affliction period for good?

10. How has God used affliction in your life to teach you about himself and his Word?

11. Of all the benefits that come from interacting with God's Word, which do you desire most in your life?

12. How can you follow the psalmist's example this week in order to receive that benefit?

13. If anything could keep you from immersing yourself in God's Word this week, what would it be?

What can you do about those obstacles?

SUGGESTED PRAYER

Ask the Lord to help you identify and overcome the distractions that keep you from taking regular time in his Word. Ask him to give you such a thirst for his Word that you are willing to take time away from something else.

MEMORY VERSE

*I have hidden your word in my heart
that I might not sin against you.*

PSALM 119:11

WALKING WITH GOD

Often we understand the benefits of God's Word but still find other things distracting us from regular Bible reading and meditation. Make a list of what often distracts you from God's Word. Then list one or two suggestions for eliminating each distraction.

If time in God's Word is not a priority in our schedules, it rarely happens. Try to determine when is the best time of your day to read the Word of God. Look at your coming week and place "time alone with God" on your daily calendar. Ask the Lord to help you keep your appointment with him. He longs to be alone with you and to share his wisdom with you.

LEADER'S NOTES

Leading a Bible discussion—especially for the first time—can make you feel both nervous and excited. If you are nervous, realize that you are in good company. Many biblical leaders, such as Moses, Joshua, and the apostle Paul, felt inadequate to lead others (see 1 Corinthians 2:3). Yet God's grace was sufficient for them, just as it will be for you.

Some excitement is also natural. Your leadership is a gift to the others in the group. Keep in mind, however, that other group members also share responsibility for the group. Your role is simply to stimulate discussion by asking questions and encouraging people to respond. The suggestions listed below can help you to be an effective leader.

1. Ask God to help you understand and apply the passage to your own life. Personal application will help you more effectively lead others.
2. Carefully work through each question in the study guide. Meditate and reflect on the passage as you formulate your answers. Beyond your own response to the passage, consider thinking of additional questions that fit or complement your group dynamic.
3. Familiarize yourself with the leader's notes for the study. These will help you understand the purpose of the study and will provide valuable background information about the questions in the study.
4. Pray for the various members of the group. Ask God to use these studies to make you better disciples of Jesus Christ.
5. Before the first meeting, make sure each person has a copy of this book. Encourage them to prepare beforehand for each study.

LEADING THE STUDY

1. Begin the study on time. If people realize that the study begins on schedule, they will work harder to arrive on time.

2. At the beginning of your first time together, explain that these studies are designed to be discussions, not lectures. Encourage everyone to participate, but realize that some may be hesitant to speak during the first few sessions.

3. Consider reading the introductory paragraph at the beginning of the discussion.

4. Read the passage aloud. You may choose to do this yourself, or you might ask for volunteers.

5. Don't be afraid of silence. People in the group may need time to think before responding.

6. Avoid answering your own questions. If necessary, rephrase a question until it is clearly understood. Even an eager group will quickly become passive and silent if they think the leader will do most of the talking.

7. Encourage more than one answer to each question. Ask, "What do the rest of you think?" or "Anyone else?" until several people have had a chance to respond.

8. Try to be affirming whenever possible. Let people know you appreciate their insights into the passage.

9. Never reject an answer. If it is clearly wrong, ask, "Which verse led you to that conclusion?" Or let the group handle the problem by asking them what they think about the question.

10. Avoid going off on tangents. If people wander off course, gently bring them back to the passage being considered. If you have difficulty staying on topic yourself, consider having someone else in the group hold you accountable.

11. Conclude your time together with prayer. Ask God to help you apply the things you learned in the study. You may also have a time for sharing some prayer requests, concerns, or praises. If the sharing period outweighs the actual prayer period, consider starting out in prayer instead of sharing. Have each person pray for themselves, lifting up all of their concerns as they feel comfortable. This may ensure that your group spends more time in prayer rather than talking or chatting.

12. End on time. This allows some in the group to leave if they feel the need. Conversation or discussion can continue after the study.

Study 1
THE GIFT OF WISDOM: 1 KINGS 3

Purpose: To discover why we should value wisdom and discernment more than riches, honor, and a long life. To ask the Lord for the gift of wisdom.

Question 1: Every study begins with a "warm-up question," which is discussed before reading the passage. A warm-up question helps to break the ice. Because a warm-up question doesn't require any knowledge of the passage or any special preparation, it can get people talking and can help them feel more comfortable with each other.

Second, a warm-up question can motivate people to study the passage at hand. At the beginning of the study, people in the group aren't necessarily ready to jump into the world of the Bible. Their minds may be on other things (their kids, a problem at work, an upcoming meeting) that have nothing to do with the study. A warm-up question can capture their interest and draw them into the discussion by raising important issues related to the study. The question becomes a bridge between their personal lives and the answers found in Scripture.

Third, a good warm-up question can reveal where people's thoughts or feelings need to be transformed by Scripture. That is why it is important to ask the warm-up question *before* reading the passage. The passage might inhibit spontaneous, honest answers because, after reading the passage, people might feel compelled to give biblical answers. The warm-up question allows them to compare their personal thoughts and feelings with what they later discover in Scripture.

Question 2: It is easy when discussing a biblical character to try to make him all good or all bad rather than seeing him as a sinner in the process of growth and change. It's important to discuss in this question how Solomon was an example of both good and compromise.

Verse 1: "This was strictly, as the language suggests, a diplomatic alliance. It reflects, moreover, the Near Eastern conception of marriage, which was an arrangement between two families, courtship being not respectable."[1]

Verse 2, *high places*: "Upon entering Canaan, the Israelites often followed the Canaanite custom of locating their altars on high hills, probably on the old Baal sites. The question of the legitimacy of Israelite worship at these high places has long been a matter of debate. It is clear that the Israelites were forbidden to take over pagan altars and high places and use them for the worship of the Lord (Numbers 33:52; Deuteronomy 7:5, 12:3). It is also clear that altars were to be built only at divinely sanctioned sites (see Exodus 20:24; Deuteronomy 12:5,8,13-14). It is not so clear whether multiplicity of altars was totally forbidden provided the above conditions were met (see [1 Kings] 19:10,14; Leviticus 26:30-31; Deuteronomy 12; 1 Samuel 9:12). It seems, however, that these conditions were not followed even in the time of Solomon, and pagan high places were being used for the worship of the Lord. This would eventually lead to religious apostasy and syncretism and was strongly condemned" (2 Kings 17:7-18; 21:2-9; 23:4-25).[2]

Verse 4, *Gibeon*: "Solomon began his reign with religious ceremonies at the important shrine of Gibeon, six miles N.W. of Jerusalem, where the tabernacle finally came to rest, and in Jerusalem itself."[3]

Verse 5: "In accordance with a custom well established in the ancient Near East, where the king was the channel of divine blessings and revelation, Solomon may have gone to the shrine of Gibeon with the express purpose of obtaining a revelation through a dream."[4]

Question 3: It is difficult to let someone make a totally open-ended request unless one trusts that person's character.

Question 5: There are several answers to this question. Solomon stated some of his reasons even *before* he made his request. Encourage the group to dig for all the answers, not just one or two.

Verse 7, *I am only a little child*: "The birth of Solomon is generally placed in approximately the middle of David's 40-year reign, meaning that Solomon was about 20 years old at the beginning of his own reign (see 2:11-12) and lacked experience in assuming the responsibilities of his office."[5]

Verse 9: "'A receptive (lit. hearing) heart' implies patience to hear a case and understand it fully. Here again there is a close parallel with Isaiah 11:3, 'he will not decide by what he hears with his ears.'"[6]

Question 8: If you have a lively, dramatic group, you could get two of your more verbal people to role-play the parts of Lawyer #1 and Lawyer #2 with someone else playing the part of Solomon.

Verses 16-28: "The final part of the chapter gives a practical example of wisdom. It is noteworthy that the king was accessible to ordinary people and that they were not slow to take advantage of their opportunity. Harlots have no great reputation for truthfulness, and it required sagacity on this occasion to effect a decision. Solomon judged rightly that the real mother of the child would be willing for the child's life to be preserved at any cost, even that of losing the right to bring it up herself, and so he gave judgment in favor of the first woman and restored the child to her."[7]

Question 12: Try to help group members focus on just one area of their lives where they need wisdom and discernment. Most of the application questions in this study guide are geared to help group members apply the passage to their lives in a very specific way. Therefore the answers to the application questions can often be used as prayer requests of each group member throughout the week. Try to help group members be specific about their applications, such as:

"I need wisdom about my nine-year-old son and how to help him achieve greater discipline with his homework."

"I need wisdom with the lady I sit next to at work—we seem to be in competition with each other rather than working as a team as we should."

Study 2
WISDOM BEYOND COMPARE: ISAIAH 55

Purpose: To desire to know and apply God's higher wisdom to our lives and let go of our own thoughts and ways.

Question 1: The invitation doesn't need to be to a party but could be an invitation to participate in a project, a class, go on a vacation, receive a promotion, and so on.

Question 2: In Isaiah 55 the prophet looks ahead to Judah's captivity in Babylon. The people were tempted to seek the comforts of Babylon rather than the "solid joys and lasting treasure" which "none but Zion's children know" all free through the covenant-grace of God.[8]

Verse 1, *no money*: "In hard times, even water had to be purchased."[9]

Verse 1, *wine and milk*: "Symbols of abundance, enjoyment and nourishment."[10]

Suggested answers for "when" on the invitation: "When you're done trying to spend money on what doesn't satisfy," or "When you're thirsty."

Verse 3, *everlasting covenant*: "David had been promised an unending dynasty, one that would culminate in the Messiah."[11]

Verse 5, *surely you will summon nations you know not*: "Although the verb is singular, it is Israel which is addressed. As in the days of David, other nations will be Israel's servants and will run to him when he summons them."[12]

Question 6: The Lord is making a direct comparison in verses 8-9 between his thoughts and ways and our thoughts and ways. Be sure that the group looks not only at verses 8-9 but also at verse 7 as they answer this question.

Question 8: "V. 11 seems to imply that God's word *does* return to him, but it does not return *empty*; that is, it achieves its purpose first and then returns to him who has spoken it. So also in Job 36:26-29 it would seem that the rain returns to heaven. This idea seems to have been dimly perceived by the ancient Israelites, even though the mechanism of evaporation was probably unknown to them."[13]

Verse 13, *cypress(or pine tree) and myrtle*: "Here we have a transformation of nature which reverses the curse upon nature pronounced in Genesis 3:18. Israel's return home will be 'Paradise Regained'. *Cypress* and *myrtle* are among the trees listed in [Isaiah] 41:19. The precise identity of the *thorn* and the *briar* is uncertain, though the context gives a general indication of their nature. In the final lines the promise is backed by a further assurance: the miraculous fertility of the desert region through which the exiles are to travel will not be a merely temporary phenomenon: the region will be preserved in that state forever as a kind of 'national park,' as a reminder not only to Israel but also to Yahweh himself, of the promise which he has made. The idea is similar to that of the establishment of the rainbow in Gen. 9:8-17 . . . and the term *shall not be cut off* . . . refers to the permanence of the sign."[14]

Question 10: Possible answers:

- My days will be more filled with joy that comes from obedience to the voice of the Lord.
- God will lead me through the maze of my unanswered

questions about my day. He will give me peace, confirming
the choices he helps me make.
- All of nature will seem to be rejoicing with me.
- Instead of my life producing thorns and briars that can harm
  me, it will produce foliage that is beautiful and that I and
  others can enjoy.

Study 3
THE BENEFITS OF WISDOM: PROVERBS 8

Purpose: To realize that God delights to give wisdom and its benefits to those who seek it.

Question 2: Throughout the Proverbs, "Wisdom" is often personified as a woman.

Verse 5, *simple*: "Denotes those who are easily persuaded or 'lack judgment' ([Proverbs] 9:4,16), who are immature, inexperienced and naive (see Psalm 19:7)."[15]

"Wisdom does not recoil from the rough and tumble of the market-place with its busyness and noise. When she raises her voice it is not to deliver an academic lecture in a classroom, or a sermon in a temple to a crowd of worshippers, or to enlighten an elite, but to summon men from their occupations and distractions to take part in an open-air meeting. She has no assurance of an audience, no prior publicity, and there are no established conventions in connection with this mode of address which guarantee that she will be treated with deference and have an easy passage.

"She operates where the competition is fiercest, not so much the competition of other orators, as men's preoccupation with those earning their living, making bargains, getting wealth, transacting local politics, settling disputes and other less gregarious enjoyments. It is against all this that Wisdom has to compete, raising her voice and summoning an audience until she wins one by sustained force of her eloquence. She picks a place where the human traffic is heaviest, whether a natural pulpit at the side of the road, or at a crossroads or beside the gates which give access to the city, where there is a continual movement to and fro and where the forum on which all manner of public transactions focus is located."[16]

Question 5: Choosing God's Wisdom begins with realizing its value: "'For wisdom is more precious than rubies, and nothing you desire can compare with her' (Proverbs 8:11). The wisdom of God is priceless, without peer. Its worth cannot be calculated. All the riches of the universe are like a beggar's hand when compared to the worth of God's wisdom."[17]

Verse 12, *prudence*: "Good judgment or good sense (see [Proverbs] 15:5; 19:25). Outside Proverbs the Hebrew word is used in the negative sense of 'shrewd' or 'crafty' (Gen. 3:1; Job 5:13)."[18]

Question 8: There are quite a few strong preferences given in these verses. Try to lead the discussion by reading each verse and looking for all the strong preferences or lofty claims listed in that verse before going on to the next verse.

Verse 13, *I hate pride and arrogance*: "The degree of wisdom we possess from God is directly proportional to our spirit of humility. A wise person is not a proud one. Pride and vanity are like poison to the spirit of wisdom. Whoever thinks he is wise is disqualified from God's classroom, where wisdom is given to the contrite of spirit and humble of heart."[19]

"Wisdom returns the love of her lovers and makes herself accessible to those who seek her."[20]

Verse 23, *from eternity*: "Descriptive also of Christ (see John 1:1; cf. Micah 5:2)."[21]

Verse 23, *before the world began*: "Wisdom was already there before God began to create the world."[22]

Verse 34, *watching daily at my doors*: "Contrast the warning not to go near the door of the adulteress's house ([Proverbs] 5:8)."[23]

Study 4
CHOOSING WISDOM OVER FOLLY: PROVERBS 9

Purpose: To realize why it is far better in life to choose wisdom rather than folly.

Question 2: verse 1, *has built her house*: "Both wisdom and folly have a house to which mankind is invited (see [Proverbs 9:]14; 7:8; 8:34), but wisdom has *built* her house . . . —for her, there is no 'sitting' (verse14).[Compare to] the virtues of the wife of noble character (31:10-27)."[24]

Verse 1, *seven pillars*: "Indicating a large house. Perhaps 'seven' refers to seven major aspects of wisdom."[25]

Question 3: For a definition of *simple* see leader's note to study 3, question 2.

Verse 4, *let all who are simple come in here*: "The young women of chapter 9 have an educational mission; they invite young men not to bed, but to school; they address themselves to the untutored youth, deficient in acumen who constitutes the raw material which the wisdom teacher shapes by an educational process. He must forsake his untutored companions and, in the face of the complexities of the world, acquire such discrimination and sagacity as will enable him to pick his steps along life's road."[26]

Question 4: Those described would probably be people who are disciplined and purposeful in their actions, just as Wisdom is as she sets her table. They would also be wise in employing the help of others, just as Wisdom, who sent out her maids.

Question 5: verse 17, *stolen water . . . food eaten in secret*: "The 'banquet' prepared by 'Folly' seems poorer than the wine and meat of wisdom (verse 2). And it was stolen at that! This 'meal' refers to stolen pleasures, exemplified by the illicit sex offered by the adulterous."[27]

Question 9: Verse 9, *instruct a wise man and he will be wiser still*: "The disciple of Christ learns and matures through Christ's discipline and chastisement. He does not pout or sulk when reproved but understands that the path of godly wisdom is his complete acceptance of God's correction and forgiveness for all his mistakes. Failures are not dead ends but valuable lessons to distill truth from error. Are you a learner? Do you hunger and thirst for righteousness? Or have you settled for a mediocre life, satisfied with a nominal knowledge of Christ?"[28]

Verse 9, *teach a righteous man and he will add to his learning*: "School is never out for true saints. They long with unceasing fervor to learn of and know Christ more intimately—the Christ in whom are hidden all the treasures of wisdom and knowledge."[29]

Question 10: This question should lead to a good discussion of times when group members have tried to correct others and have been met with various responses. It could also lead to discussion about when group members have themselves been corrected and how they personally responded to instruction or rebuke.

Study 5
GOD'S PROMISED GUIDANCE: PSALM 32

Purpose: To discover that God's hand is still on us even when we sin and choose to go our own way, as well as when God is weaving the silver and gold threads into the pattern of our lives.

Question 2: verse 1, *blessed*: "'Happy,' a more exuberant word than 'blessed,' is the proper opening to both these beatitudes (verses 1 and 2)."[30]

Verse 2, *in whose spirit is no deceit*: "Only those honest with God receive pardon."[31]

Question 3: verse 4, *hand was heavy upon me*: "If forgiveness is good, fellowship is better; if we have experienced God's heavy hand (verse 4), we should appreciate and seek His gentler touch."[32]

Questions 4–5: It is often easier to identify symptoms or problems in others first before claiming them as our own. Encourage good discussion on question 4 as people identify physical symptoms in others. It may take some vulnerability on your part for group members to be willing to share honestly their own physical symptoms due to deceit or unconfessed sin.

Question 5 can lead to greater group understanding and open an opportunity for practical support and prayer for those dealing with various physical symptoms. Avoid implying that physical symptoms are always connected to sin.

Question 6: "His confession of sin implied his repentance; for the fact that he speaks with candour of his sin as sin and confesses his guilt as such makes sense only on the assumption that he truly repents of his sins and longs for a clean heart. How he feels that he is relieved of the burden which pressed heavily upon him and tormented him; now peace has entered his soul, and he can again freely lift up his eyes to his God. Turning his thoughts to God and experiencing the deliverance wrought in his heart, he discovers that God has forgiven him the guilt of his sin."[33]

Question 8: Verse 6, *mighty waters*: "Powerful imagery for threatening forces or circumstances."[34]

Verse 7, *surround me with songs of deliverance*: "Because of your help, I will be surrounded by people celebrating your acts of deliverance, as I bring my thank offerings to you."[35]

There seem to be two different methods of hiding which the psalmist describes in this psalm—trying to hide or cover over our sin (verse 1), and hiding in God (verse 7). Because these different types of hiding are found in verses 1 and 7, it is easy to miss the contrast.

Question 9: "This vivid picture brings out, by its contrasts, the emphasis of verse 8 on intelligent co-operation, which God has set His heart on eliciting from us; for whatever else one can do with a horse one can hardly counsel it, or control it without bringing pressure on it. Jeremiah 8:6 uses it to picture a more forceful waywardness than that of the proverbial sheep: 'Everyone turns to his own course, like a horse plunging headlong into battle' [ESV]."[36]

Question 11: This question can enable people to be honest about past times of rebellion. The emphasis of the discussion, however, should be on how God sovereignly used circumstances in people's lives as "bit and bridle" to rein in their stupidity or rebellion. You may need to be vulnerable first before others feel free to share.

Question 13: There may be many areas where we all need God's guidance, but encourage people to focus on just one. This way the answers to this question can become a prayer list for group members during the week.

Study 6
GOD'S BOOK OF WISDOM: PSALM 119:9-16,65-72

Purpose: To be motivated to appreciate the availability of God's Word and all its richness.

Question 2: verse 10, *I seek you*: "The author's devotion is first of all to the God of the law and the promises; they have meaning for him only because they are God's word of life for him."[37]

Verse 9, *young man*: "From the heartfelt prayers of the surrounding verses it would seem that the *young man* is the psalmist himself in the first place. He is praying rather than preaching." [38]

Verse 11, *hidden your word in my heart*: "Proverbs 2:10-12 and

Colossians 3:16 show that the mind which stores up Scripture has its taste and judgment educated by God."[39]

Question 3: It is good to be reminded of the benefits of God's Word, but perhaps it's even more important to see that we can only experience those benefits if we are aggressively interacting with the Word of God ourselves. Since this is the final study in this guide, what a great opportunity to encourage group members to continue their study of the Word on a regular basis. That takes initiative on our part.

Question 5: Answers to this question might include:

- Both bring initial immediate happiness, but the happiness of riches dies quickly, such as when we get a new shirt or sweater that quickly becomes old.
- Both bring status from other people. Those who obey Christ are often greatly respected within the church, and those who have wealth are respected in the community. But obedience to God's Word brings an internal respect as well that comes from knowing you are in fellowship with God.

Question 8: verse 66, *judgment*: "literally 'taste,' not in our sense of artistic judgment, but of spiritual discrimination; 'for the ear tests words as the palate tastes food.' [Verses 67,71] Expresses the psalmist's gratitude for bitter medicine. He is even grateful for the affliction which was needed to bring him to heel. As for the rest of his sufferings, they are well outweighed by the 'great spoil' he has found in God's word."[40]

Question 12: As in previous application questions, help group members to take one specific step, such as:

- "I need to get up a half hour earlier to spend time in God's Word."
- "I need to work on memorizing Scripture, one verse per week, so that I have it 'hidden' in my heart."
- "I need to give the Lord my best hour of the day, which is when the kids nap, and entrust the rest of my day to him."

These "steps" can then be used as prayer requests as the group prays for one another.

NOTES

Chapter 1: The Gift of Wisdom

1. The Encyclopedia of 7700 Illustrations (Rockville, MD: Assurance Publishers, 1979), 1612.

Chapter 4: Choosing Wisdom over Folly

1. Charles Stanley, *A Touch of His Wisdom* (Grand Rapids, MI: Zondervan, 1992), 41.

Leader's Notes

1. John Gray, I and II Kings, The Old Testament Library (Philadelphia, PA: The Westminster Press, 1970), 118.
2. The NIV Study Bible (Grand Rapids, MI: Zondervan, 1984), 476.
3. I. Howard Marshall, I Kings–II Chronicles, Scripture Union Bible Study Books (Grand Rapids, MI: Eerdmans, 1967), 9.
4. Gray, 124.
5. The NIV Study Bible, 476.
6. Gray, 126.
7. Marshall, 9.
8. Arthur E. Cundall, Isaiah 40–Jeremiah, Scripture Union Bible Study Books (Grand Rapids, MI: Eerdmans, 1969), 19.
9. The NIV Study Bible, 1097.
10. The NIV Study Bible, 1097.
11. R. N. Whybray, Isaiah 40–66, The New Century Bible Commentary (Grand Rapids, MI: Eerdmans, 1981), 192.
12. Whybray, 192.
13. Whybray, 194.
14. Whybray, 195.
15. The NIV Study Bible, 946.
16. William McKane, Proverbs, The Old Testament Library (Philadephia, PA: The Westminster Press, 1970), 344–345.

17. Stanley, 41.
18. The NIV Study Bible, 946.
19. Stanley, 45.
20. McKane, 350.
21. The NIV Study Bible, 926.
22. The NIV Study Bible, 926.
23. The NIV Study Bible, 957.
24. The NIV Study Bible, 957.
25. The NIV Study Bible, 957.
26. McKane, 360.
27. The NIV Study Bible, 957.
28. Stanley, 46.
29. Stanely, 45.
30. Derek Kidner, Psalms 1–72, *Tyndale Old Testament Commentaries* (Downers Grove, IL: InterVarsity, 1973), 133.
31. The NIV Study Bible, 816.
32. Kidner, Psalms 1–72, 134.
33. Kidner, Psalms 1–72, 285.
34. The NIV Study Bible, 816.
35. The NIV Study Bible, 816.
36. Kidner, Psalms 1–72, 135.
37. The NIV Study Bible, 915.
38. Derek Kidner, Psalms 73–150, *Tyndale Old Testament Commentaries* (Downers Grove, IL: InterVarsity, 1973), 424.
39. Kidner, Psalms 73–150, 424.
40. Kidner, Psalms 73–150, 426, 423.

Enjoy these other titles from the WALKING WITH GOD series.

We all long for an intimate relationship with our heavenly Father. The Walking with God series was created to foster a deeper knowledge and understanding of who He is. Each book focuses on a singular attribute of God, such as His power and wisdom. The studies are warm, practical, and personal, yet firmly grounded in scriptural truths.

Our Faithful Friend

John Sloan

ISBN-13: 978-1-57683-620-0

ISBN-10: 1-57683-620-7

God longs for an intimate relationship with each of us. But what does it mean to be friends with the Lord? This study highlights a God who can always be trusted and who is forever faithful.

Our Loving Father

Jack Kuhatschek

ISBN-13: 978-1-60006-219-3

ISBN-10: 1-60006-219-9

God's love is infinite in measure. No one loves more deeply or forgives more readily. This insightful study explores God's endless love and encourages readers to model His perfect example.

Our Powerful Helper

Marshall Shelley

ISBN-13: 978-1-57683-627-9

ISBN-10: 1-57683-627-4

God's power is made perfect in our weakness. This study shows readers that He can be trusted in all circumstances and that His wondrous power is made available to us through prayer.

Visit your local Christian bookstore, call NavPress at 1-800-366-7788, or log on to www.navpress.com to purchase.
To locate a Christian bookstore near you, call 1-800-991-7747.

NAVPRESS®